JUL 3 1 2017

**WOODS BRANCH
GROSSE POINTE PUBLIC LIBRARY
GROSSE POINTE, MI 48236**

Really Strange Adaptations

Really Strange
MAMMALS

Janey Levy

PowerKids press
New York

Published in 2017 by The Rosen Publishing Group, Inc.
29 East 21st Street, New York, NY 10010

Copyright © 2017 by The Rosen Publishing Group, Inc.

All rights reserved. No part of this book may be reproduced in any form without permission in writing from the publisher, except by a reviewer.

First Edition

Editor: Theresa Morlock
Book Design: Reann Nye

Photo Credits: Cover, p. 1 (mammal) Joel Sartore, National Geographic Photo Ark/National Geographic/Getty Images; cover (inset background), p. 27 (sea lion) Andrea Izzotti /Shutterstock.com; cover, pp. 1–32 (background) Iakov Kalinin/Shutterstock.com; p. 4 bondburn/Shutterstock.com; p. 5 (mouse) Rudmer Zwerver/Shutterstock.com; p. 5 (giraffe) Anna Levan/Shutterstock.com; p. 5 (moose) Richard Seeley/Shutterstock.com; p. 5 (hippo) Eduard Kyslynskyy/Shutterstock.com; p. 5 (cat) Vitaliy Hrabar/Shutterstock.com; p. 6 claupad/Shutterstock.com; p. 7 Worraket/Shutterstock.com; p. 8 Troutnut/Shutterstock.com; p. 9 (naked mole rat) Frans Lanting/Mint Images/Getty Images; p. 9 (rock hyrax) Bartosz Budrewicz/Shutterstock.com; p. 10 TOM MCHUGH/Science Source/Getty Images; p. 11 Tier Und Naturfotografie J und C Sohns/ Photographer's Choice/Getty Images; p. 12 Auscape/Universal Images Group/Getty Images; p. 13 (vampire bat) Michael Lynch/Shutterstock.com; p. 13 (solenodon) Nicholas Smythe/Science Source/Getty Images; p. 13 (short-tailed shrew) John Macgregor/Photolibrary/Getty Images; p. 13 (slow loris) Visuals Unlimited, Inc./Thomas Marent/Visuals Unlimited/Getty Images; p. 13 (platypus) worldswildlifewonders/Shutterstock.com; p. 14 Vladimir Wrangel/Shutterstock.com; p. 15 Shchipkova Elena/Shutterstock.com; p. 16 (okapi) Eric Isselee/Shutterstock.com; p. 16 (zebra) Patryk Kosmider/Shutterstock.com; p. 17 ZSSD/Minden Pictures/Getty Images; p. 19 Visuals Unlimited, Inc./Ken Catania/Getty Images; p. 20 Erni/Shutterstock.com; p. 21 Alex Sotelo/Moment/Getty Images; p. 22 Andre Coetzer/Shutterstock.com; p. 23 Daryl Balfour/Gallo Images/Getty Images; p. 24 (male) uzuri/Shutterstock.com; p. 24 (female) Richard Whitcombe/Shutterstock.com; p. 25 Fiona Rogers/Corbis Documentary/Getty Images; p. 27 (beluga whale) Christopher Meder/Shutterstock.com; p. 27 (manatee) Liquid Productions, LLC/Shutterstock.com; p. 27 (bottlenose dolphin) Willyam Bradberry/Shutterstock.com; p. 27 (sea otter) Menno Schaefer/Shutterstock.com; p. 28 Vadim Petrakov/Shutterstock.com; p. 29 Pacific Press/LightRocket/Getty Images; p. 30 (Amazon river dolphin) guentermanaus/Shutterstock.com; p. 30 (aye-aye) javarman/Shutterstock.com; p. 30 (agouti) Andrew M. Allport/Shutterstock.com; p. 30 (wombat) Robyn Butler/Shutterstock.com.

Cataloging-in-Publication Data
Names: Levy, Janey.
Title: Really strange mammals! / Janey Levy.
Description: New York : PowerKids Press, 2017. | Series: Really strange adaptations | Includes index.
Identifiers: ISBN 9781499427899 (pbk.) | ISBN 9781499428483 (library bound) | ISBN 9781508153009 (6 pack)
Subjects: LCSH: Mammals–Miscellanea–Juvenile literature.
Classification: LCC QL706.2 L49 2017 | DDC 599–dc23

Manufactured in the United States of America

CPSIA Compliance Information: Batch #BW17PK: For Further Information contact Rosen Publishing, New York, New York at 1-800-237-9932

CONTENTS

MARVELOUS MAMMALS 4
NOT ALWAYS SO WARM-BLOODED 6
THE PECULIAR PLATYPUS 10
THE GIRAFFE'S COUSIN 14
IT CAME FROM ANOTHER WORLD 18
POPCORN-PERFUMED PEE? 20
THE PREHISTORIC PANGOLIN 22
THE IMPROBABLE PROBOSCIS MONKEY 24
DIVING MAMMALS' AMAZING ADAPTATION . . . 26
MORE AND MORE MARVELOUS MAMMALS . . . 28
GLOSSARY 31
INDEX 32
WEBSITES 32

MARVELOUS MAMMALS

We live in what's called the Age of Mammals. After the large dinosaurs died out 65 million years ago, mammals became the dominant animals. Humans are mammals. So are dogs, cats, horses, squirrels, mice, goats, giraffes, hippos, bears, deer, moose, and many more animals.

Mammals live in nearly every **biome**, from deserts to rain forests to oceans. To flourish in all these **environments**, they've developed a wide array of adaptations. For example, mammals living in very cold climates may have thick fur and a layer of fat. Some adaptations are amazing and strange. Some are even mysterious. Did you know scientists still aren't sure why zebras have stripes? Keep reading to learn more!

FAMILIAR MAMMALS, AMAZING ADAPTATIONS

If you've ever watched dogs, you know they're always sniffing at things. That's because they learn about the world mostly through smell. Their sense of smell is 10,000 to 100,000 times better than ours. They can even detect the terrible disease called cancer by smell! What about cats? Cats have one of the broadest hearing ranges of all mammals. They need only one-sixth as much light as you do to see clearly.

Mammals occupy every continent. Scientists believe that there are about 5,400 species of mammals in the world today.

NOT ALWAYS SO WARM-BLOODED

When we list the features that make an animal a mammal, one feature we include is being warm-blooded. That means mammals are able to maintain a high and fairly constant body temperature no matter what the temperature of their surroundings might be.

red fox
mammal

Being warm-blooded uses a lot of energy. Some mammals have adapted to allow their body temperature to go down at times to conserve energy. Some do it seasonally, during winter **hibernation**. Some do it daily, when they go into a state called **torpor** while sleeping. A few mammals have found that the benefits of conserving energy outweigh the benefits of maintaining a constant body temperature.

While mammals are warm-blooded, reptiles are cold-blooded. That means their body temperature depends on their surroundings. They don't need as much energy—food—to stay alive.

iguana
reptile

Arctic ground squirrels drop their core, or center, body temperature below freezing during hibernation, yet they never freeze solid. The common blossom bat of Australia, Indonesia, and New Guinea has a normal body temperature of 96.8° Fahrenheit (36° Celsius) during the night, when it's active. However, during daily torpor, the bat allows its body temperature to drop—all the way down to 68° Fahrenheit (20° Celsius)! The pygmy mouse lemur of Madagascar lets its body temperature drop even lower. It goes below 44.6° Fahrenheit (7° Celsius) and can stay there about 10 hours a day!

A scientist studied one hibernating Arctic ground squirrel that dropped its core body temperature to 26.8° Fahrenheit (–2.9° Celsius)! Water freezes at 32° Fahrenheit (0° Celsius).

rock hyrax

naked mole rat

LIKE LIZARDS

Rock hyraxes are squat, furry mammals found across Africa and the Middle East. Like naked mole rats, they can't control their body temperature well. However, they spend time out in the open, not just in tunnels. So how do they keep warm? Like lizards, they stretch out in the sun to warm up in the morning. Their homes are dens, where they pile on top of each other to conserve body heat.

Naked mole rats don't control their body temperature very well. However, they don't need to since they spend their entire life in underground tunnels where the temperature is usually between 84.2° Fahrenheit (29° Celsius) and 89.6° Fahrenheit (32° Celsius).

THE PECULIAR PLATYPUS

The platypus—sometimes called the duck-billed platypus—is one of the world's oddest mammals. It belongs to a small group of mammals called monotremes, which are native to Australia.

Monotremes don't have a stomach. How weird is that?

The platypus is so odd that when a dead one was shipped to British scientists in the 1790s, they thought it was fake. Who can blame them? The platypus has an otter's furry body, a beaver's paddle-shaped tail, a duck's webbed feet, and a soft, moist variation of a duck's bill. Even odder, platypuses lay eggs instead of giving birth to live young. They also have a skeleton that resembles that of a reptile. Some scientists even consider them to be reptiles, not mammals—although they'd be pretty odd reptiles, too!

ANOTHER MONOTREME

The short-beaked echidna uses its impressive snout, or beak, to locate prey: ants, termites, and earthworms. The rubbery beak not only smells prey, it also detects the tiny electrical signals produced by the prey's body. Once the echidna finds food, its sharp claws tear open the prey's mounds or nests and its long, sticky tongue captures the prey. But the echidna's most remarkable adaptation is the way it survives Australia's frequent wildfires. It goes into torpor in its underground burrow and sleeps through them!

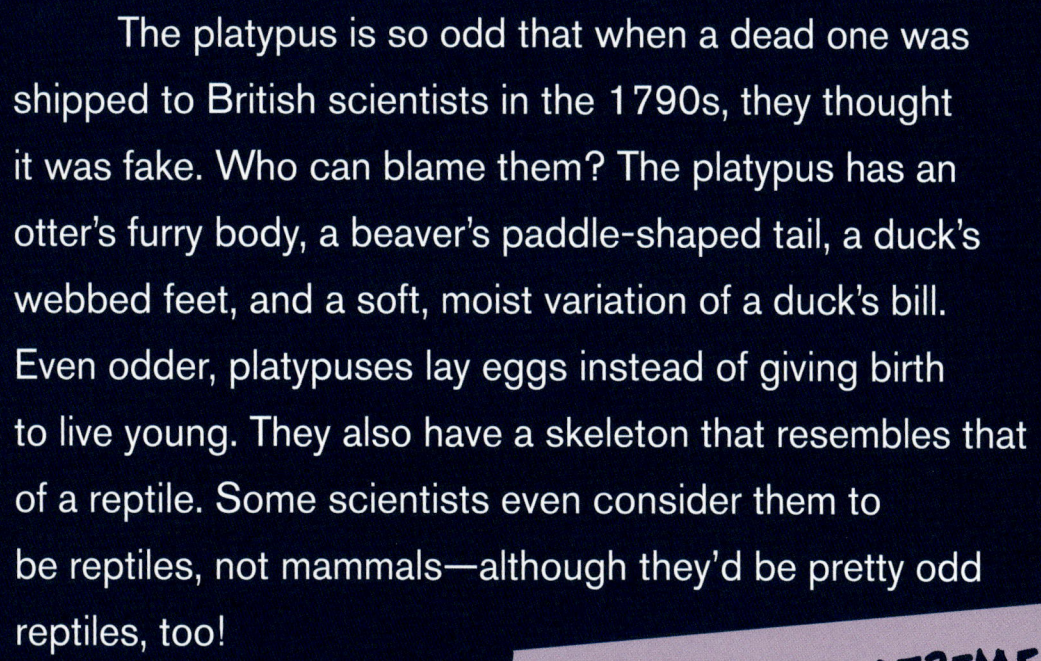

11

As odd as platypuses look, they're perfectly adapted to their environment and way of life. They hunt for food in freshwater rivers, streams, ponds, and lakes. They swim with their front feet and steer with their back feet and tail. Their fur keeps them warm. Skin covers their eyes and ears while they're underwater, and their nose seals shut. So how do they find prey? Their bill has **electroreceptors** that detect the tiny electrical signals sent out by the muscle movements of their prey!

Male platypuses have another special adaptation. They have spurs on their back feet connected to a gland that produces **venom**. They're one of the few venomous mammals in the world. They use their venom against predators and in fights with other males during mating season.

venomous spur

VENOMOUS MAMMALS

VAMPIRE BATS
venom keeps victims' blood from clotting

SLOW LORISES
venom causes swelling, loss of fur, and death

some SHREWS AND SOLENODONS
venom causes the victim to be unable to move and to have trouble breathing

short-tailed shrew

solenodon

PLATYPUSES
venom causes swelling, breathing problems, clotting of blood inside blood vessels, and death

13

THE GIRAFFE'S COUSIN

Its front legs and rear end are dark with white stripes, somewhat like a zebra. But if you look closely at its head and watch its tongue pull leaves from trees, you realize it resembles a giraffe. In fact, it's the giraffe's only living relative. It's the okapi (oh-KAH-pee). While giraffes live in herds on the African savanna, okapis live alone in the African rain forest.

Okapis can eat up to 65 pounds (29 kg) of leaves, twigs, and fruits daily using their tongue, which can be up to 18 inches (46 cm) long. They also use their tongue to groom their own eyes, ears, and nose!

Okapis have many adaptations to help them live safely in their rain forest home. Though they live alone, they have ways of communicating with each other. Scent glands on their feet leave a sticky, tar-like substance wherever they walk, marking their territory. They "talk" to each other often, but some of their calls are too low to be heard by people—and predators.

THE GIRAFFE'S NECK

It's long been said that giraffes developed long necks as an adaptation to help them reach leaves in treetops. However, scientists found giraffes generally feed with their necks bent. Even during the dry season, when there's more competition for food, giraffes feed from low shrubs rather than treetops. Some scientists now believe the long necks developed because males use them when fighting for mates and males with longer necks usually win. Also, female giraffes seem to prefer males with longer necks.

Okapis' dark, reddish-brown fur with white stripes helps them blend into the sun-streaked darkness of the rain forest and hide from predators. The fur is also oily, so water slides right off on rainy days, keeping okapis nice and dry.

THE ZEBRA'S STRIPES

Scientists have long argued about why zebras have stripes. One of the main theories is that the stripes provide camouflage. Others believe the stripes may protect zebras from biting flies. The number of stripes on a zebra usually relates to the temperature of the area it lives in. Zebras in warm areas have big bold stripes that cover their bodies, while those in colder temperatures have fewer stripes and none on their legs. This suggests that a zebra's stripes help it control its body temperature.

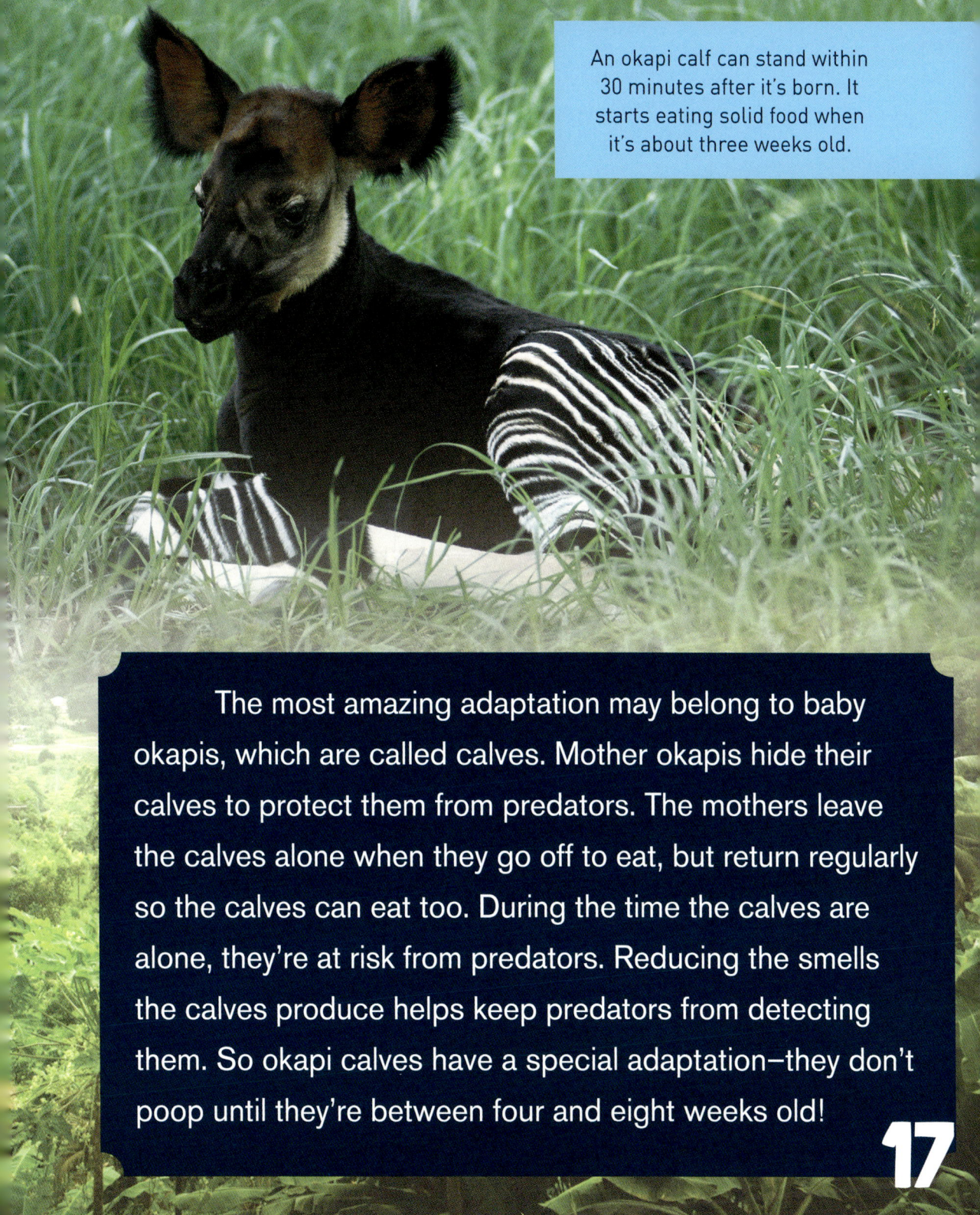

An okapi calf can stand within 30 minutes after it's born. It starts eating solid food when it's about three weeks old.

The most amazing adaptation may belong to baby okapis, which are called calves. Mother okapis hide their calves to protect them from predators. The mothers leave the calves alone when they go off to eat, but return regularly so the calves can eat too. During the time the calves are alone, they're at risk from predators. Reducing the smells the calves produce helps keep predators from detecting them. So okapi calves have a special adaptation—they don't poop until they're between four and eight weeks old!

IT CAME FROM ANOTHER WORLD

A star-nosed mole looks like a creature from another world, and, in a sense, it is. Its world is underground and along the bottom of **wetlands**, and it's perfectly adapted to its life there.

The star-nosed mole's broad front feet, with their long claws, are excellent for digging burrows. Because it lives and **forages** in dark places, its eyesight is poor. But it has the perfect adaptation for finding food: that strange-looking star-shaped nose.

The mole's nose is made up of 22 **tentacles**, called rays. Each tentacle is covered by small touch-sensitive structures called Eimer's organs. These structures enable the mole to identify an object, decide if it's prey, and eat it in just one-quarter of a second! That's astounding!

Because these mammals spend their lives underground and along wetland bottoms, there's still much scientists don't know about them.

BLOWING BUBBLES

Scientists recently discovered that star-nosed moles rapidly blow bubbles out their nose when they're underwater. Then they immediately suck the bubbles back into their nose. Why? They're blowing the bubbles at specific objects. When the bubbles touch an object, they pick up odors from it, and when the moles suck the bubbles back into their nose, they're able to detect the odors. In other words, they're using the bubbles to smell and help them find prey underwater!

POPCORN-PERFUMED PEE?

Its proper name is the binturong, but it's also known as the bear cat because its face resembles a cat's and its body resembles a bear's. Although it's officially a carnivore, it eats mostly fruit. The binturong lives in the rain forests of Southeast Asia, where it spends most of its time high in the trees. One adaptation that helps with its treetop life is its prehensile tail. "Prehensile" means "adapted for grasping," and binturongs use their tail like another hand.

Binturongs make lots of noises to communicate. They snort, wail, howl, grunt, and hiss. They even laugh!

But the binturong's oddest adaptation is the odor of its pee. It smells like buttered popcorn! Binturongs use their pee to mark their territory and attract mates. But it's hard to say why it smells like popcorn rather than something else.

21

THE PREHISTORIC PANGOLIN

The pangolins of Asia and Africa look like creatures that might have walked with dinosaurs—and they did! They've been around for over 80 million years. They're the only scaly mammals, and their scales are just one of their amazing adaptations.

DINING WITH PANGOLINS

Pangolins have poor eyesight, so they locate ant and termite nests with their sense of smell. After they tear the nests open, they use their extremely long, sticky tongue to scoop up the insects. A single pangolin can eat 70 million insects a year! Pangolins have no teeth, so they can't chew. But their stomach is muscular and lined with spines to crush their prey. Pangolins also swallow stones to help grind up their prey in their stomach.

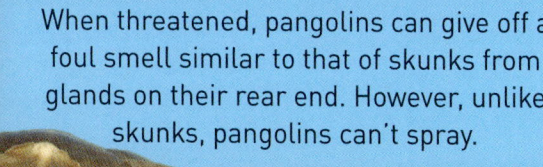
When threatened, pangolins can give off a foul smell similar to that of skunks from glands on their rear end. However, unlike skunks, pangolins can't spray.

Pangolin scales are made of keratin, which is the same protein that forms human hair and nails. The scales overlap, like artichoke leaves, and protect the pangolin like armor. When threatened, a pangolin rolls up in a ball, and even a lion can't bite through the scales!

Pangolins have strong legs and three long, curved claws on each front foot. They use their powerful front legs and claws to tear open the nests of the ants and termites they eat. The claws are actually strong enough to dig through concrete!

THE IMPROBABLE PROBOSCIS MONKEY

The forests of Borneo, an island in Southeast Asia, are home to an unusual monkey known as the proboscis monkey. A proboscis is a very long nose. The nose is one of the most noticeable features of male proboscis monkeys. Males—and only males—have a large, **pendulous** nose that hangs down over their mouth.

Why do male proboscis monkeys have this unusual adaptation? Scientists are unsure. They think it may create a kind of echo chamber that makes the monkey's call louder, impressing females and frightening rival males.

male

female

Proboscis monkeys live in groups made up of a mature male and two to seven females and their young. Several groups may come together at dusk to rest, and rival males may make noisy displays at such times.

Proboscis monkeys eat leaves, seeds, and unripe fruit. They don't eat ripe fruit because the sugars in it can **ferment** in their stomach and kill them.

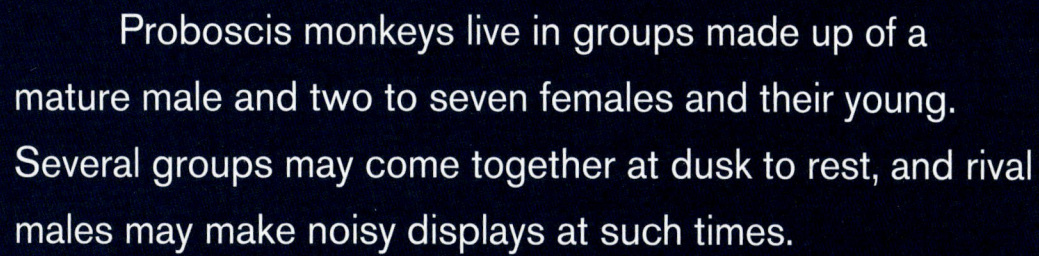

HITTING THE WATER

Proboscis monkeys are excellent swimmers and sometimes leap from trees into rivers below. Their dive can be very funny, since they hit the water with their stomach first in a belly flop. But swimming has its risks, since crocodiles lurk in the rivers. Proboscis monkeys have developed an adaptation that helps them swim fast to escape the crocodiles: They have webbed hands and feet!

25

DIVING MAMMALS' AMAZING ADAPTATION

Diving mammals such as whales, seals, and even beavers often stay underwater for extended periods. How do they do it? Scientists have discovered an amazing adaptation having to do with an oxygen-carrying protein called myoglobin found in their muscles.

All mammals have myoglobin. But myoglobin is 10 times more concentrated in the muscles of diving mammals than in human muscles. If humans had that much myoglobin, the proteins would stick together, causing serious health problems. The myoglobin proteins in diving mammals don't stick together. All that extra myoglobin allows diving mammals to keep a large store of oxygen to use while they're underwater. That's an awesome adaptation!

MORE DIVING MAMMAL ADAPTATIONS

Besides all that myoglobin and stored oxygen, diving mammals have many other adaptations that help them make lengthy dives. They can slow their heart rate, stop their breathing, and direct their blood flow to their most important body parts—brain, heart, and muscles. Those adaptations are pretty impressive, too. They allow elephant seals to stay underwater for two hours.

All diving mammals have extra myoglobin, whether they live in salt water or freshwater.

sea lion

manatee

beluga whale

bottlenose dolphin

sea otter

27

MORE AND MORE MARVELOUS MAMMALS

The strange and wonderful mammal adaptations you've read about are just a few of the many that exist. The world is full of remarkable mammals with impressive adaptations, and more are being discovered all the time.

Capybaras, which live in Central and South America, are the world's largest **rodents**, weighing up to 174 pounds (79 kg)! They spend much of their time in water and have adaptations for that lifestyle, including webbed feet like a duck or frog.

Tarsiers cling to tree branches and use their strong lower legs to jump. Tarsiers can jump distances of up to 40 times the length of their body!

Indonesia's Siau Island tarsiers are one of the smallest known **primates**. They hunt insects at night and have adaptations to help with that. Their head can turn almost completely around, and their huge eyes, designed to take in as much light as possible, can weigh more than their brain!

MAMMAL FAST FACTS

AYE-AYE

Largest nocturnal primate. An aye-aye has huge, leathery ears that help it locate prey. It also has long, thin, third fingers on each hand, which are used to pull insect larvae from trees.

AMAZON RIVER DOLPHIN

One of few freshwater dolphin species. They're often pink, and scientists disagree about why.

WOMBAT

Australian marsupial. When threatened, a wombat dives into its burrow and blocks the entrance with its rear end. The skin on its rear end is so thick that it won't be bothered by a bite there!

AGOUTI

Rodent from Central and South American rain forests. It has such a keen sense of hearing that it can hear when falling fruit—its favorite food—hits the ground.

30

GLOSSARY

biome: A natural community of plants and animals, such as a forest or desert.

electroreceptor: An animal body part that can detect electrical signals.

environment: The conditions that surround a living thing and affect the way it lives; the natural world in which a plant or animal lives.

ferment: To change a sugar or starch into an alcohol or acid in the absence of oxygen.

forage: To search for food.

hibernation: A sleep-like state an animal may enter for an extended period of time, usually during winter.

pendulous: Drooping.

primate: Any mammal of the group that includes humans, apes, and monkeys.

rodent: Any mammal of the group that includes rats, mice, and beavers.

tentacle: A long, thin body part that sticks out from an animal's head or mouth.

torpor: A state of heavy sleep in which animals lower their body temperature and reduce their energy use to get through short periods.

venom: Something an animal makes in its body that can harm other animals.

wetland: Land containing much moisture in the soil, such as a swamp, marsh, or bog.

INDEX

A
Africa, 9, 14, 22
agouti, 30
Asia, 20, 22, 24
Australia, 8, 10, 11, 30
aye-aye, 30

B
bat, common blossom, 8
bat, vampire, 13
binturong, 20, 21

C
cats, 4
capybara, 28
Central America, 28, 30

D
dogs, 4
dolphin, Amazon river, 30
dolphin, bottlenose, 27

E
echidna, short-beaked, 11

G
giraffe, 4, 14, 15

H
hyrax, rock, 9

L
lemur, pygmy mouse, 8
loris, slow, 13

M
manatee, 27
marsupial, 30
mole, star-nosed, 18, 19
mole rat, naked, 9
monkey, proboscis, 24, 25
monotremes, 10, 11

O
okapi, 14, 15, 16, 17
otter, sea, 27

P
pangolin, 22, 23
platypus, 10, 11, 12, 13
primate, 29, 30

R
rodent, 28, 30

S
sea lion, 27
shrew, 13
solenodon, 13
South America, 28, 30
squirrel, Arctic ground, 8

T
tarsier, 29

W
whale, beluga, 27
wombat, 30

Z
zebra, 4, 16

WEBSITES

Due to the changing nature of Internet links, PowerKids Press has developed an online list of websites related to the subject of this book. This site is updated regularly. Please use this link to access the list: www.powerkidslinks.com/rsa/mamm